THE BOXCAR CHILDREN

by
Gertrude Chandler Warner

Teacher Guide

Written by
Monica L. Odle

> **Note**
> The paperback edition of this book, published by Albert Whitman & Company, ©1942, was used to prepare this guide. Page references may differ in other editions.
>
> **Please note:** Please assess the appropriateness of this book for the age level and maturity of your students prior to reading and discussing it with your class.

ISBN 1-58130-730-6

To order, contact your local school supply store, or—

Copyright 2002 by Novel Units, Inc., San Antonio, Texas. All rights reserved. No part of this publication may be reproduced, stored in a retrieval system, or transmitted in any way or by any means (electronic, mechanical, photocopying, recording, or otherwise) without prior written permission from the publisher, with the following exceptions: Photocopying of student worksheets by a classroom teacher at a non-profit school who has purchased this publication for his/her own class is permissible. Reproduction of any part of this publication for an entire school or for a school system or for commercial sale is strictly prohibited. Copyright infringement is a violation of Federal Law.

Novel Units is a registered trademark of Novel Units, Inc.

Printed in the United States of America.

PAPERBACKS - BMI BOUND BOOKS
TEACHER'S GUIDES - AUDIO-VISUALS
PO BOX 800 - DAYTON, N.J. 08810-0800
Toll Free Phone 1-800-222-8100
America's Finest Educational Book Distributor

Table of Contents

Summary 3

About the Author 3

Initiating Activities 3

Vocabulary Activities 4

Thirteen Chapters 11
    Each section contains: Summary,
    Vocabulary, Discussion Questions,
    and Supplementary Activities

Post-reading Discussion Questions 23

Post-reading Extension Activities 24

Assessment 27

Skills and Strategies

Thinking
Compare/contrast, research, brainstorming, analysis

Writing
How-to, poetry, creative, narrative, descriptive, recipes, songs

Listening/Speaking
Discussion, oral presentation, drama, small group/partner interaction

Comprehension
Decision-making, pros/cons, predictions, evaluation

Vocabulary
Definitions, compound words, spelling, application

Literary Elements
Plot, point of view, characterization, setting, figurative language

Across the Curriculum
Social Studies—geography, heritage; Math—word problems; Science—research, plants, time line; Art—collage, drawing, design, puppets; Health—field day, diet/nutrition

Summary

Four children, Henry, Jessie, Violet, and Benny, are orphaned after their parents' death. Rather than live with a grandfather they do not know, they find shelter in a boxcar in the woods. The children self-sufficiently turn the boxcar into a comfortable home and adopt a dog they name Watch. Henry finds a job working at the home of Dr. Moore and his mother in Silver City. Dr. Moore soon discovers that the children's grandfather is the wealthy Mr. Alden. When Violet gets sick and the children stay at Dr. Moore's home while she is nursed back to health, the children meet a lovable man they later learn is their grandfather. The four Alden children go to live with Mr. Alden who cares for them. Because they sometimes miss their old home in the boxcar, Mr. Alden has it transported from the woods outside of town to his own yard.

About the Author

Gertrude Chandler Warner was born in Putnam, Connecticut, on April 16, 1890, across the road from a railroad station. She was a first-grade teacher for 32 years. She published her first book, *House of Delight*, in 1916. While recuperating from an illness, Warner began wondering what living inside a train was like. This led to the writing of the Boxcar Children series, the first of which was published in 1924, and then again in 1942, revised with simpler language. Warner wrote 18 more of the Boxcar Children stories (48 exist in the series today). She died in her hometown on August 30, 1979.

Initiating Activities

1. Creative Writing: With the class, brainstorm a list of chores students must do at home or in the classroom. Allow each student to pick a chore from the list and then compose a poem or short story about an imaginary character who loves to do that chore. The students should give their character a funny name associated with the chore (i.e., Lori Lawnmower or Larry Laundry). Set aside time for the students to read their stories and poems to the class. If time allows, instruct the children to illustrate their story or poem.

2. Previewing the Book: Read the first paragraph of the story and any book jacket information. From these readings and from looking at the title and cover of the book, have the students write a paragraph predicting what the book will be about.

3. Prediction: Ask if the students have read any other books in the Boxcar Children series. Discuss how other books are alike and different and try to predict what the first book in the Boxcar Children series will be like.

4. Anticipation/Opinion: Have students decide whether or not they agree with the following statements. Record their responses. Read their responses again after reading the book and see if anyone's opinion changes.

- All children have homes to live in.
- Children should never be allowed to live on their own.
- It is important to have a positive attitude about hard work.
- Chores are fun.
- It is not important to get along with brothers and sisters.

Vocabulary Activities

1. Teaching in Pairs: Place students in pairs. Give them the list of vocabulary words for each section after they have finished reading it. Each pair should alphabetize the words and divide the list in two. Each person must look up the definition for his or her half of the words in a dictionary. Allot class time for the students to teach their partners the words they have each defined.

2. Flash Cards: Provide note cards for each student. Have them write a vocabulary word on one side and the part of speech, pronunciation, and definition on the other side. For homework, have the students review the words once each night at home with their parents, guardians, or another study partner.

3. Compound Words: Have students pick out all of the compound words from the vocabulary list. Then, have them write sentences using the two base words and the compound word. (Example: "horseshoe"; I accidentally kicked the *horse* in the ribs with my *shoe* when I was riding him to get his *horseshoes* repaired.)

4. Spelling/Definition Bee: Conduct a spelling bee with your class using vocabulary words. Once the students are skilled at spelling the words, conduct the spelling bee as a definition bee, where students must define each word correctly to continue from one round to the next.

5. Cartoons: Have the students draw cartoon pictures that express the definition of each word. The pictures can depict objects, actions, or even use dialogue to express a feeling. However, the students should not be allowed to write the actual vocabulary word on the picture. Display some student samples on the classroom bulletin board.

6. Draw the Definition: Play a game where the students are divided into two teams. One person from Team 1 comes to draw the definition of a vocabulary word they choose from a hat. If Team 1 guesses the correct word, they get a point. If not, they lose the point and it is the other team's turn to draw. Continue playing for points until all words are used. If a team drawer does not know the definition, he or she may consult the other team for three possible definitions. One of the three options provided by the opposing team must be correct. The team with the most points wins. Teachers can make this an ongoing game, adding points as each section of the book is read and the game is played with new words.

7. **Word Maps:** Have the students complete a word map for three vocabulary words from each section. Have them keep their word maps in a folder in alphabetical order. Before any vocabulary tests or quizzes, divide the class into small groups and allow them to use their word maps as review sheets.

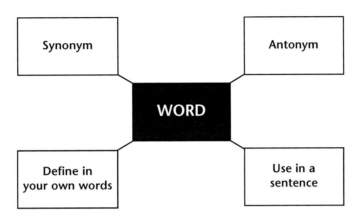

Prediction Chart

What characters have we met so far?	What is the conflict in the story?	What are your predictions?	Why did you make those predictions?

Story Map

Setting

Characters _____
_____

Time and Place _____
_____

Problem

Problem _____
_____
_____

Goal

Goal _____
_____

Beginning ⟶ Development ⟶ Outcome

Episodes

_____
_____
_____
_____

Resolution

Resolution _____
_____
_____
_____

Attribute Web

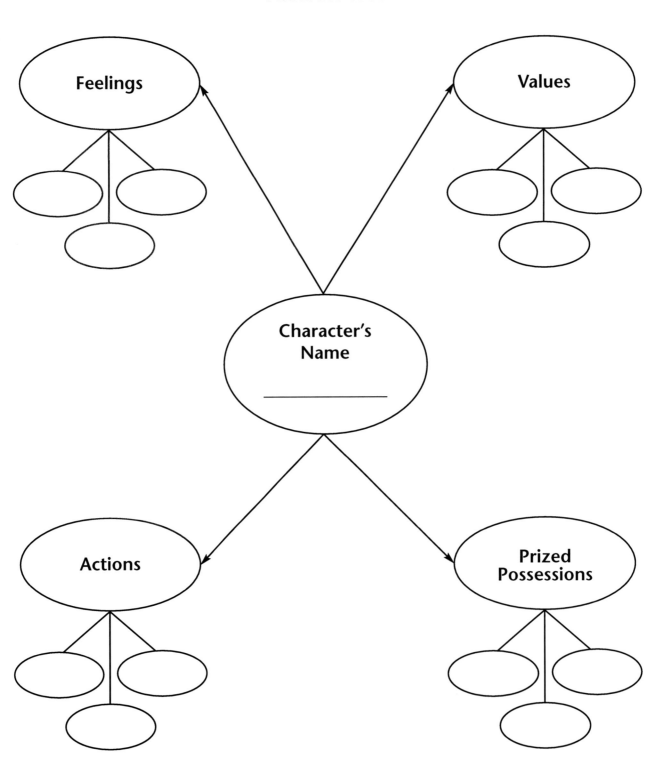

Value Chart

Values represent people's beliefs about what is important, good, or worthwhile. For example, most families consider spending time together as very important—it is something they value.

Directions: Think about the following characters from *The Boxcar Children*. What do they value? What beliefs do they have about what is important, good, or worthwhile? On the chart below, list each character's three most important values, from most important to least. Be prepared to share your lists during a class discussion.

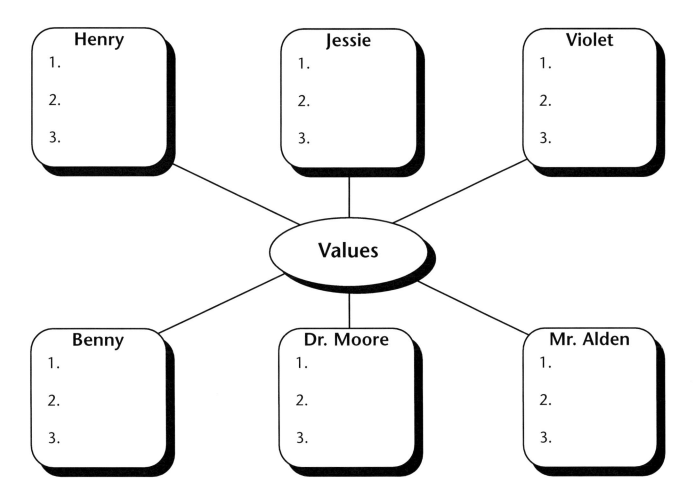

Venn Diagram

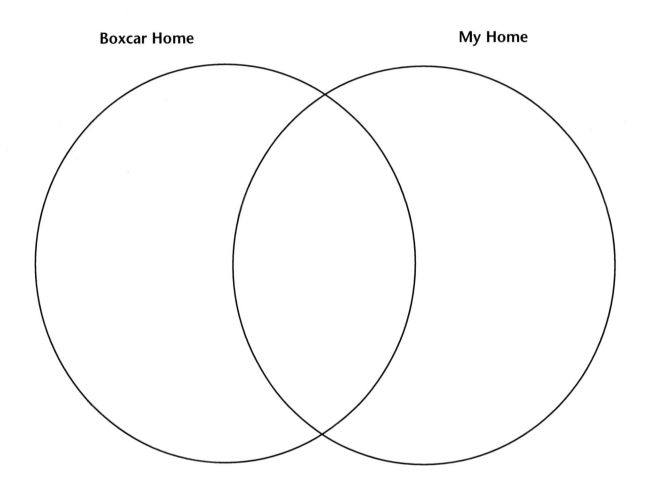

Chapters I-II, pp. 7-26

Four children, Henry, Jessie, Violet, and Benny, whose parents have died, try to find food and shelter for a night at a bakery. Upon overhearing the baker and his wife planning to keep three of them and take the fourth to a Children's Home, they escape in the night. The baker and his wife look for them, but do not find them, and the children look for a good place to live and hide from the baker, his wife, and the grandfather they have never met.

Vocabulary

bakery (7)	loaves (8)	politely (9)	delicious (11)
whispered (13)	laundry (13)	farmhouses (18)	haystack (18)
brook (18)	pump (20)	listen (23)	fountain (24)
pine needles (25)			

Discussion Questions

1. What is the tone of the first paragraph of the story? Why? *(Answers will vary; mysterious; It is night and no one knows anything about the children standing in front of the bakery.)*

2. How many children are there? What are their names? *(four; Henry, Jessie, Violet, Benny)*

3. How are the children related? *(They are brothers and sisters.)*

4. Why don't they have a home? *(Their parents died and they don't want to live with their grandfather.)*

5. What are the children doing at a bakery? *(buying bread for dinner)*

6. Why do they ask to spend the night at the bakery? *(Answers will vary; they do not have a place to live.)*

7. Where do the children want to sleep? *(on long, red benches under the bakery windows)*

8. Why does the woman let the children spend the night? *(They offer to help her wash dishes.)*

9. Do the children sleep the whole night at the bakery? Why or why not? *(No; they overhear the baker and his wife talking about sending Benny to a Children's Home and decide to leave so that they can stay together.)*

10. What is a Children's Home? *(Answers will vary; probably an orphanage; a homeless shelter for children)*

11. When the children leave the bakery, where do they go? *(They walk until they find a place to sleep in a haystack.)*

12. How do the children eat and drink? *(They still have bread; they find a water pump at a farmhouse and pump water to drink.)*

13. Why do the children decide to go to Silver City? *(The baker and his wife are going to look for them in Greenfield.)*

14. How do the children find their way to Silver City? *(They follow the street signs.)*

15. What do the children see on the side of the road? *(The road is deserted, but they do find a water fountain with many different drinking levels.)*

16. Where do the children sleep that night? Why? *(They sleep in the woods because the woods are far away from people and close to the fountain; they sleep on pine needles for beds.)*

17. Why do the children sleep so deeply that they do not even hear the storm? *(The children are tired because they walked all night until 2:00 a.m. and have not had much to eat.)*

18. **Prediction:** What will happen to the children since it is thundering and there is lightning?

Supplementary Activities

1. Research: Have students research pine needles and their many uses. Encourage them to collect pictures of pine needles if they find any, and display them on a classroom bulletin board. Help them understand how pine needles can be used to make a bed.

2. Geography: The four children follow signs to get to Silver City. Have the students draw a map of their own school. Give each student one hallway for which they must design signs to direct strangers to places in the school such as the office, cafeteria, library, etc. If you have permission, let the students post their signs in the hallways. See page 26 of this guide for a template.

3. Art: Have students illustrate the impending storm using watercolors or oil pastels.

Chapters III-IV, pp. 27-44

The children find an old, abandoned boxcar in the woods and decide to live there. Henry goes to a nearby town to find food while the children discover a wandering, injured dog. Jessie cleans the dog's wound, and Benny names the dog "Watch." The children continue to make the boxcar a home.

Vocabulary

thunder (28)	boxcar (28)	track (28)	rusty (28)
beginning (29)	stump (29)	climbed (29)	lightning (30)
engine (31)	softly (35)	thorn (35)	handkerchief (36)
bundles (38)	watchdog (39)	tablecloth (40)	blueberries (40)
clothesline (42)	towel (43)		

Discussion Questions

1. What is the weather like when the children wake up the next morning? What do the children do? *(It is windy and stormy. It starts to rain, and the children look for shelter.)*

2. What is a boxcar? Who finds it? *(part of a train where cargo is kept; Jessie)*

3. Do you notice anything special about the order in which the children enter the boxcar (p. 29)? *(Answers will vary; it seems that they enter in order of age, indicating that Benny is the youngest, then Violet and then Jessie. Henry is probably the oldest.)*

4. What are the reasons the children decide to live in the boxcar? *(It is in a "beautiful place," and it is dry, warm, near a brook, and abandoned.)*

5. How do the children know a train engine will not come to take the boxcar away? *(The grass is overgrown onto the boxcar; the track is old and rusty.)*

6. What are the children eating for dinner? Why does Henry go into town? *(bread; to buy milk)*

7. What two things do the children find in the woods? *(blueberries and a dog)*

8. Who takes care of the dog's thorn injury? *(Jessie)*

9. What is the dog's new name? Why does Benny choose that name? *(Watch; They decide the dog is a watchdog.)*

10. What are in Henry's heavy bundles when he returns from town? *(four bottles of milk, brown bread, yellow cheese)*

11. What do the children mean when they say "dinner" and "supper"? *(Dinner is the midday meal [lunch]; supper is the evening meal.)*

12. Why does Violet tell Benny to pretend to be Little Brown Bear? *(Answers will vary; Benny doesn't like to wash, and Violet knows that if he pretends to be a bear, he will like bathing.)*

13. Why does Henry go to the fountain to get water? *(He can hide if anyone comes along. The children are still hiding from their grandfather.)*

Supplementary Activities

1. Math: The children eat blueberries and milk with their dinner. Have students calculate the answers to the following word problems. Then have them write two of their own word problems and calculate the answers.

    - If the children eat 30 blueberries each, how many blueberries will they eat in all? *(120 blueberries)*
    - If the children have four bottles of milk and drink half, how much milk is left? *(2 bottles)*
    - If the loaf of bread is divided equally between Henry, Jessie, Violet, Benny, and Watch, what fraction of the bread does each one get? *(1/5 of a loaf)*

2. Music/Oral Reading: Play music in the background that sounds like rain or another form of water (brook, storm, etc.). Then read the beginning of Chapter III aloud. Call on students to continue reading Chapter III aloud to the same background music. Allow students to listen or quietly draw pictures of what they are visualizing.

3. Descriptive Writing: Provide a picture of a boxcar from a train. Then have students write a description of the children's home in the woods.

Chapters V-VI, pp. 45-68

Henry goes into Silver City to find a job while the other three children go exploring for treasures at a dump. They find dishes, four wheels, and a shelf for the boxcar. Henry returns home with a new job working for a doctor and many new bundles. That night, Watch, Henry, and Jessie hear someone walking in the woods.

Vocabulary

housekeeper (45)	waterfall (46)	refrigerator (46)	treasures (47)
explorers (48)	pitcher (51)	carefully (52)	admired (52)
suddenly (53)	hem (61)	growl (66)	frightened (66)

Discussion Questions

1. What are the children using as a refrigerator? *(a hole behind the waterfall)*

2. Why does Henry go into town? *(to find work so that the children can eat)*

3. What is ironic about Jessie's plans for the day? *(She wants to look for treasures at a dump. "Treasures" and "dump" have two different meanings—treasures are valuable and the items thrown away at a dump are worthless.)*

4. Why do you think Benny wants to find wheels at the dump? *(Answers will vary.)*

5. Who finds the treasures first? *(Benny)*

6. What do the children find at the dump? Why do they consider these items to be treasures? *(a white pitcher, a white cup, a teapot, two other cups, bowls, five rust-covered spoons, a pink cup with a handle, four matching wheels; These items are things the children don't need to survive, but that will make their life more comfortable.)*

7. How do the children keep the dishes in the boxcar? *(They make a shelf from a board they find at the dump.)*

8. Why does Jessie want to clean the dishes with soap, sand, and hot water? *(The soap and sand clean the rust and the dirt, and hot water kills any germs that are still on the dishes.)*

9. What does Henry bring back from town? *(funny-looking bundles containing bread, milk, dried meat, and a bone for Watch; a job working for a doctor)*

10. How does Henry find a job? *(He sees a man mowing his yard and asks if he can mow it instead. He does such a good job that the man, who is a doctor, asks Henry to come work for him the next day as well.)*

11. What does the doctor's house look like? *(It is big with a yard, garage, vegetable garden, and cherry orchard.)*

12. What does the cook give to Henry? *(cookies)*

13. What two projects do the girls work on that day? What does Benny do? *(The girls hem a tablecloth and make a broom while Benny finds sticks for the broom, plays with Watch, and falls asleep.)*

14. What do the children have for supper? *(dried meat, bread and butter, cookies, and milk)*

15. What do the children want to build next? How? *(a swimming pool by damming up the brook)*

16. How would you describe these four children? *(Answers will vary; polite, mature, self-sufficient, thankful, etc.)*

17. Why doesn't Watch fall asleep right away? *(He hears a noise outside.)*

18. **Prediction:** Who or what is in the woods that night?

Supplementary Activities

1. Creative Writing: The children are called "explorers" when they go to look for treasures (p. 48). Have students write a story in which they are explorers searching for a treasure of some kind.

2. Science: Have students research rust and draw pictures or write a paragraph explaining how rust develops and how it affects humans if it is ingested.

3. How-to Writing: Instruct students to reread the section of the book where Benny, Jessie, and Violet make a broom. Then, have them write a composition telling how to make a broom. Another option is to have students illustrate the process and include captions.

Chapters VII-VIII, pp. 69-92

Henry works thinning Mrs. Moore's (the doctor's mother's) vegetable garden. Later in the day he cleans the garage and Dr. Moore gives him a hammer. The other three children construct a "building" (fireplace) where they make stew for supper that night. On Sunday, the four of them build a swimming pool at the brook and find hen eggs in the woods.

Vocabulary

queer (69)	rabbit (70)	vegetables (71)	turnips (72)
mill (72)	indeed (73)	eager (74)	wire (74)
fireplace (75)	garage (76)	stirred (79)	ladle (79)
cart (80)	remarked (80)	dam (81)	admired (82)
delighted (85)	laid (87)		

Discussion Questions

1. Why aren't Henry and Jessie worried about the noise they heard in the woods the night before? *(Watch pays close attention to the noises in the woods. He is a good watchdog who loves the children and will protect them if there is any danger.)*

2. What precautions do the children take after they hear someone in the woods? *(Jessie decides to keep Violet, Benny, and Watch by her at all times and not let them go into the woods alone.)*

3. What does Henry do for Mrs. Moore during the morning? What does she give him when he is done? *(He thins out her vegetable garden. She allows him to keep the vegetables he pulled and pays him one dollar.)*

4. What is the building that Jessie, Violet, and Benny are so proud of when Henry returns to the boxcar for dinner? How did the children and Watch make it? *(a fireplace; Watch dug a hole which Benny lined and surrounded with stones while the girls hung a kettle on a wire they tied between two trees.)*

5. What are the children having for dinner? How are they cooking it? *(stew; boiling meat in a kettle over the fire; They will put vegetables in after the meat cooks awhile, and will add salt when Henry comes home that night.)*

6. Why does Violet fill a pitcher and teapot with water? *(to put on Benny or Watch if they catch on fire)*

7. What does Henry do for the remainder of the day for Dr. Moore? What does he receive for his work? *(He cleans the garage and is paid another dollar. He is also given a hammer and some bent nails.)*

8. Why does Dr. Moore continue to ask Henry to work for him? *(Answers will vary.)*

9. Why is Henry concerned about building the swimming pool on a Sunday? *(Answers will vary; Sundays are traditionally days when businesses close, some religious services are held, and people rest rather than work.)*

10. What do Benny and Henry make with Benny's wheels? *(a cart)*

11. Why does Benny fall asleep with his hand on his cart and Henry fall asleep with his new hammer under his pillow? *(Answers will vary.)*

12. How deep is the pool by the brook that Jessie had seen? *(one foot deep)*

13. How do the children build a dam to make a swimming pool? *(with boards, stones, and brush)*

14. Why is Henry concerned that the pool be deep enough to swim in but not "too deep for Benny" (p. 85)? *(Answers will vary; Henry is protecting Benny from being in water so deep that he might drown.)*

15. What are some reasons why the children seem to like working hard? *(Answers will vary; because they get satisfaction when they see the finished product or can buy something with the money they earn, etc.)*

16. How do the children find hen eggs in the woods? *(They go exploring after they eat and Watch finds a hen nesting. After Watch chases the hen away, the children discover the eggs.)*

17. Who finds the eggs? *(Benny)*

18. **Prediction:** What else will the children have to eat besides bread and milk the next day? How will they get different food?

Supplementary Activities

1. Brainstorming: Discuss the children's attitude toward work. Have the class think about other stories or movies where people are excited about their work (*Snow White*, etc.). On a T-chart, list students' responses to the pros and cons of working hard.

2. Math: Have students answer the following word problems. Then allow students to make up their own word problems regarding depth and distance. They should also provide the answer to each word problem they write.

    - Henry says that the one-foot deep pool needs to be three times deeper so they can swim in it. How deep does the pool need to be? *(three feet deep)*
    - If the pool was only six inches deep, how much deeper would it need to be to reach a depth of three feet? *(3.0 / 0.5 = 6 times deeper, or 3 feet – 1/2 foot = 2 1/2 feet deeper)*
    - How deep would the pool be if it were three times deeper than three feet? *(nine feet deep)*

3. Science: Just as the children in the story build a dam, so too do beavers. Arrange a library visit for students to do research on beavers. They can also research famous human-built dams. Students should write a research report on their findings and give an oral presentation to the class, complete with visual aid, on how dams are built or how they function.

Chapters IX-X, pp. 93-116

The four children work in the cherry orchard at Dr. Moore's house. Dr. Moore discovers that they are the grandchildren of the wealthy James Henry Alden, who sponsors Field Day in Silver City. Henry runs in the free-for-all race, and earns the silver trophy and $25 from Mr. Alden, who does not know Henry is his grandson. Meanwhile, Jessie and Violet teach Benny to read.

Vocabulary

ought (94)	ladders (95)	laughed (96)	orchard (96)
dumplings (97)	enough (98)	thousand (99)	prizes (102)
bleachers (103)	trained (104)	potatoes (111)	

Discussion Questions

1. Why isn't Henry sure that all four of the children should help pick cherries at Dr. Moore's orchard? *(The children are still hiding from their grandfather. People looking for them will probably be looking for a group of four children.)*

2. How do Jessie and Henry solve the problem of being seen as a group of four? *(They will go to Dr. Moore's house in pairs. Henry and Benny will go first, and the girls will follow with Watch so Watch can track the scent to the house.)*

3. Why do you think Watch barks at Jessie when she climbs up the tree on a ladder? *(Answers will vary.)*

4. How do the children enjoy picking cherries? *(Answers will vary; They seem to enjoy it very much because Mrs. Moore says they are "happy cherry pickers" and they get to eat a cherry every now and then.)*

5. Why does Dr. Moore ask the children if their mother will be looking for them? *(Answers will vary; He suspects that the children do not live with their parents.)*

6. How does Jessie respond? Why does she respond this way? *(Instead of lying, she tells the doctor that their parents are dead; Answers will vary.)*

7. What does Dr. Moore discover that night after the children leave? *(Henry, Jessie, Violet, and Benny are James Henry Alden's grandchildren.)*

8. What is the reward Mr. Alden offers to anyone who can find the children? Why does Dr. Moore decide not to tell Mr. Alden that he knows where his grandchildren are? *($5,000; Answers will vary.)*

9. What do we know about J. H. Alden? *(He is the children's grandfather, is very wealthy, and hosts a Field Day in Silver City every year.)*

10. Why does Dr. Moore take Henry to Field Day? *(Answers will vary; He wants to give Henry an opportunity to meet his grandfather without either of them knowing it.)*

11. What race does Henry win? What is his prize? *(the free-for-all; a silver trophy and $25)*

12. Why do you think Henry wins the race when he didn't train for it like all of the other runners did? *(Answers will vary. Note that Henry says he is running because it is fun. When he runs for the prize money, he is thinking as much about his siblings as he is himself.)*

13. Why doesn't Dr. Moore tell Henry that he saw the free-for-all race? *(Answers will vary.)*

14. What does Jessie decide Benny needs to do? What do the girls wish they had? *(learn to read; a book)*

15. Does Benny want to learn to read at first? What makes him want to read? *(He doesn't want to read at first, but when he thinks that Watch is learning to read faster, he is determined to learn.)*

16. How do the children remedy the problem of not having a book? *(They make one from paper left over from the bundles, using the end of a burned, black stick to write.)*

17. **Prediction:** What do you think the doctor will do in Chapter XI titled, "The Doctor Takes a Hand"?

Supplementary Activities

1. Art: Dr. Moore sees a "lost" ad that Mr. Alden put in the newspaper. Tell students to assume that Mr. Alden knows what his grandchildren look like. Have them design a "lost" flyer for the children. The students should include any important information (i.e., if there is a reward and how much, contact information, etc.) as well as their own depiction of each child.

2. Health/Sports: Allot time to take the class outside to a place where they can run safely. Then, have the class run a race or participate in other events that might occur during a field day. Give a small prize to the winner of each event.

3. Literacy/Writing: Have students make a book like Jessie and Violet do in the story. The book should focus on teaching someone how to read. Encourage the students to be creative and use simple words at first and more difficult words towards the end.

Chapter XI, pp. 117-127

Henry continues to work for the doctor, Jessie and Violet make Benny a toy bear from his old stockings, and Benny gives Watch a haircut. Violet gets sick and Henry seeks help from Dr. Moore. The doctor takes all of the children to his house while Violet is nursed back to health. Mr. Alden comes to Dr. Moore's house to meet his grandchildren, but does not tell them who he is at first because they are scared of their grandfather.

Vocabulary

stockings (118)	workbag (118)	tail (118)	scissors (119)
hospital (122)	pillows (124)	crossly (124)	quietly (126)

Discussion Questions

1. What new things does Benny get? *(a new pair of stockings and a new bear made out of his old stockings)*

2. What is unique about Benny's bear? Why does Benny like it that way? *(It has a long, thin tail; He can pull the bear easily.)*

3. What does Jessie do to Benny? What does she use? *(cuts his hair with Violet's scissors)*

4. What does Benny do to Watch? *(cuts his hair [fur] in the shape of a "J" for "Jessie")*

5. Why do Jessie and Violet cry when they see Watch? *(They are laughing so hard they cry because Watch looks funny—usually dogs don't get their hair cut with scissors by a five-year-old.)*

6. Why doesn't Violet stop crying? *(She gets sick.)*

7. How do the children take care of Violet? *(Jessie makes her go to bed and Henry goes to get the doctor. They discuss going to the hospital but decide against it because they do not want to give their names there.)*

8. How does Dr. Moore know where the children live without Henry telling him where to go? *(Answers will vary.)*

9. What does the doctor do for Violet at his house? *(He gives her a warm bed and sits by her side all night because she is so sick.)*

10. Who is the man that comes to the house the next morning? *(Answers will vary; He is looking for his lost boy about Benny's age and wants to give the doctor $5,000.)*

11. How does Benny respond to the visitor? *(He likes him and volunteers to go with him if the other little boy doesn't appear.)*

12. What does Dr. Moore tell the visitor? What doesn't he tell the children? Why? *(that Benny and the other children in the house are his grandchildren; The children do not know that the visitor is Mr. Alden, their grandfather, because Dr. Moore knows they are afraid of their grandfather.)*

13. What does Mr. Alden call his oldest grandson when Dr. Moore hints at who he is? *(the running boy)*

14. **Prediction:** Will the children learn to like their grandfather and want to live with him?

Supplementary Activities

1. Writing/Point of View: Show students how the story is written in the third-person omniscient point of view, where the narrator can comment on every aspect of the story. Using other examples, show them how a story written in first-person is different. Have students reread the section where Benny cuts Watch's hair and rewrite it from Watch's point of view.

2. Geography: The children consider taking Violet to a hospital when she gets sick. Divide the class into small groups and give each group a map of the city or area of the city where they attend school. Ask each group to locate the nearest hospital, fire department, and police station. Then have them write directions from the school to each location. They should use the directions "north," "south," "east," and "west" and use correctly determined distances based on the map's scale whenever possible.

Chapters XII-XIII, pp. 128-154

Mr. Alden stays with Dr. Moore until his grandchildren discover who he is. Mr. Alden visits the children's boxcar home in the woods. The children move into Mr. Alden's house and each get their own room, but still miss the boxcar. A man comes to claim Watch, but the children are eventually allowed to keep him. Mr. Alden moves the boxcar to his own yard as a surprise for his grandchildren.

Vocabulary

grandchildren (128)	grandfather (129)	cucumber (130)	flowers (132)
patted (132)	excited (135)	daytime (137)	pleased (139)
arrived (140)	sniffed (140)	another (148)	afraid (150)
homesick (151)	kettle (151)		

Discussion Questions

1. What do Mrs. Moore, Dr. Moore, and Mr. Alden discuss? *(that the children will not want to go with Mr. Alden until they learn to like him; Mrs. Moore invites Mr. Alden to stay with them for a while and Dr. Moore refuses to accept the reward money for finding the children.)*

2. Why is Mary afraid to cook for Mr. Alden? *(Mr. Alden is very rich and she is afraid he won't like her food.)*

3. Why does Henry recognize Mr. Alden? *(Henry remembers him from the free-for-all race.)*

4. Why do the children like Mr. Alden? *(He is kind to them and tells interesting stories.)*

5. What does Mr. Alden bring Violet when he can finally see her? *(flowers from his garden)*

6. How does Henry find out that Mr. Alden is his grandfather? *(He asks Dr. Moore for the name of the man who gave him the prize at the free-for-all. Dr. Moore tells Henry that he was J. H. Alden of Greenfield.)*

7. How do the children react when they find out who their grandfather is? Why? *(They are excited; he is not what they expected.)*

8. When did Mrs. Moore and Dr. Moore see the boxcar? *(Dr. Moore saw it the first night after Henry worked for him because he followed Henry home. The day the children went to pick cherries, both Dr. and Mrs. Moore went out to the boxcar at different times to look around and make sure the children had enough food.)*

9. What do the children show Mr. Alden? *(They take him to see their home at the boxcar. They show him everything they built and found.)*

10. Do the children want to see their grandfather's house and live with him there? What is his house like? *(yes; The house is beautiful and full of flowers and maids. Each child gets his or her own room.)*

11. How does Mr. Alden redecorate the rooms? *(He puts violets in Violet's room; animal wallpaper, a rocking horse, toolbox, and train in Benny's room; and a bed for Watch in Jessie's room.)*

12. Who is at the door? What is going to happen to Watch? *(someone saying that Watch belongs to him; Answers will vary.)*

13. Why can't the man let the children keep the dog? What must they do to keep Watch? *(He sold the dog to another lady. The children must ask the lady if she will take another dog instead of Watch.)*

14. What does Mr. Alden do when the young lady says she can have a different dog? *(He pays the man for Watch.)*

15. Why do the children laugh at the dinner table that night? *(Watch has his own chair.)*

16. Judging from Mr. Alden's clues, what is the surprise he plans to give his grandchildren? *(He hints that the surprise isn't pretty and is heavy. Answers will vary.)*

17. What is the surprise? Why do the children like it so much? *(Mr. Alden moves the boxcar to his backyard; Answers will vary.)*

Supplementary Activities

1. Characterization: Ask students how the children's perception about their grandfather changes from the beginning of the story to the end. Have them use a T-chart to sort their ideas.

Beginning	End

2. Heritage: Henry James Alden is named after his grandfather, James Henry Alden. Ask the students if they are named after anyone in their families. If so, they should interview a parent or the family member they are named after and write a report about that person. If they are not named after someone, have them find out where their name (first or last) comes from and write a report about the origin of their name and its meaning(s).

3. Analysis/Writing: As a class, brainstorm a list of characteristics evident in fairy tales. Based on the last line of *The Boxcar Children*, assess whether or not this story is a fairy tale. Then, have students write down their opinion, supporting their position with specific examples from the book.

Post-reading Discussion Questions

1. How will the children's lives be different now that they are living with their grandfather?

2. What do you think it would feel like to be homeless?

3. How would *The Boxcar Children* be different if Henry never met Dr. Moore?

4. Judging from their personalities and skills, what do you think life was like for Henry, Jessie, Violet, and Benny before their parents died?

5. Use a Venn diagram to compare and contrast the children's home in the boxcar to their home at Mr. Alden's house.

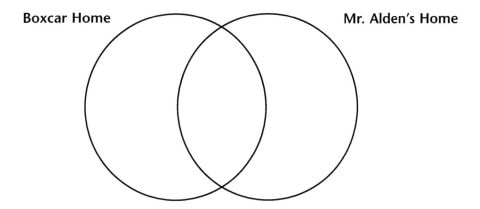

6. What part or parts of the story didn't you like? Why not? Explain how and why you would change them if you were the author.

7. Discuss how the children made different things while living in the woods. What kinds of things would you like to make from nature? Explain how you would make those items.

8. How realistic is this story? What beliefs does the reader have to suspend to enjoy this book?

9. When was this book first published? Do you think the story would be different if it were written about children today? Why or why not?

10. What lessons do the children learn by running away from the adult who is supposed to take care of them? How did living on their own benefit the children? What benefits are there when they live with their grandfather?

Post-reading Extension Activities

1. Have students write a poem that personifies Stockings the bear.

2. *The Boxcar Children* is set in the country and in a small town. Have students write a summary of this same story indicating how it would be different if the children were in a big city. Here are a few ideas as to what questions their summaries should answer:
   - What city would they live in?
   - Where would they live?
   - How would they find work?
   - Would they find a dog?
   - Would their grandfather ever find the children?

3. Have students write a haiku about a pet they have or would like to have. The haiku can be about Watch from *The Boxcar Children* if they prefer. (A haiku is a three-line poem with 17 syllables and it does not have to rhyme. The first line has five syllables, the second line has seven, and the third line has five syllables.)

4. Ask students to choose their favorite food from home. Have them write down the name of the food and its recipe. Let them come up with their own version of the recipe, just remind them of the important parts of recipes such as an ingredients list and any mixing or cooking instructions. After each student returns his/her recipe, photocopy them so that each student receives a copy of every recipe. Help students bind the pages together so that they can take home their class' very own recipe book.

5. Divide the class into small groups that will make puppets for each main character in the book. Each group will perform a puppet show for the class that covers one section of *The Boxcar Children*. (Some groups may need to make puppets for minor characters, too, depending on which section the group chooses.)

6. Allow the class to decorate a big box to put in a corner of the classroom. Label the box "Donations" and have the students bring to school things they think a homeless child might like or need, such as toys, books, clothes the students have outgrown, or something the students make as a gift. Take the donations to a children's homeless shelter in your town. If you receive permission, inspire the class to get their entire grade or school involved in donating items. They can make advertisements using persuasive strategies to post around the school.

7. Have students do a research project on the plants in their area. Each student should find one plant that is poisonous and one that is edible. The students will be graded on an oral report they give telling their classmates about each plant. Each student should bring pictures or pieces of the edible plant (some type of visual aid) so that the other students can see what the poisonous and edible plants look like.

8. Have students write a song about *The Boxcar Children* to the tune of their own favorite song. They may tape-record the song or perform it for the class.

9. Have each student make a menu of all of the items the Alden children eat while they are in the woods. Ask students to analyze whether or not the children have a good, healthy diet. Then, have each student amend his or her menu so that it provides the proper portions of each food group every day. Remind them to add only the items they think the children could find (or afford to buy) while living in the woods.

10. Divide the class into small groups and give each group three packets of different kinds of seeds. Have each group create a planting schedule based on the information provided on the packages and their knowledge of the community's climate. Each group should also indicate how much water and sun each type of seed needs to survive and when they should be harvested. If feasible, let the class plant their seeds outside and see if their schedules accurately depict how best to grow the seeds.

11. Develop a lesson where the class investigates or is taught about where the water they drink comes from. Teach students facts about water sources such as aquifers, irrigation pipes, and nearby bodies of water. Explain how drought or excessive rainfall affects local water sources.

12. As a class, investigate where the garbage in your community goes. Research to find out how full the local landfill is, how much garbage people produce each year, and where garbage must go when the landfill is completely full. Then, have students think about what they can do to reduce garbage production. This may involve learning more about local recycling programs.

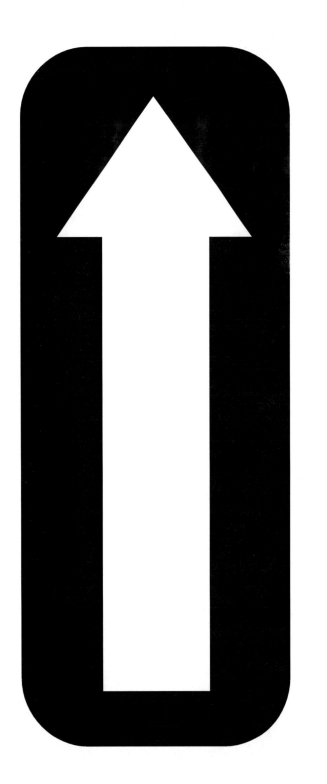

Assessment for *The Boxcar Children*

Assessment is an ongoing process. The following ten items can be completed during the novel study. Once finished, the student and teacher will check the work. Points may be added to indicate the level of understanding.

Name _____ Date _____

Student   **Teacher**

_____   _____   1. Write a description of Dr. Moore using similes, metaphors, and other colorful, descriptive language.

_____   _____   2. Make a collage for one of the characters in the book. Do not put the person's name on the collage, but make it evident through the use of pictures which character the collage represents.

_____   _____   3. Make a time line for how long the children live on their own. Use indicators in the book, such as when they sleep and how many days they work. Make good guesses to fill out places in your time line where the book isn't specific. Then, compare your time line to a classmate's time line. Discuss how and why your time lines are the same or different.

_____   _____   4. Develop attribute webs for Benny and Jessie.

_____   _____   5. Evaluate the decisions the children make while living in the boxcar. Make a list of things that you would do differently and tell how and why you would make those choices.

_____   _____   6. Use your imagination to fill out the attribute web on page 8 of this guide for the children's mother and father.

_____   _____   7. Think of another adventure the Boxcar Children could have and then develop an outline for another book about Henry, Jessie, Violet, Benny, Watch, and Mr. Alden.

_____   _____   8. With a small group, act out one of the sections in the book.

_____   _____   9. Fill out the Venn diagram on page 10 of this guide comparing and contrasting the children's home in the boxcar with your own home.

_____   _____   10. Write a story about an adventure that you had by yourself or with other children your age. Be specific and use dialogue when possible. Refer to *The Boxcar Children* for examples about how to write dialogue if necessary.

© Novel Units, Inc.   All rights reserved

Notes